What, Me Pregnant?

Other For Better or For Worse ® Books

A For Better or For Worse Collection

What, Me Pregnant?
by Lynn Johnston

Andrews and McMeel
A Universal Press Syndicate Company
Kansas City

ISBN: 0-8362-1876-0
Library of Congress Catalog Card Number: 91-73167

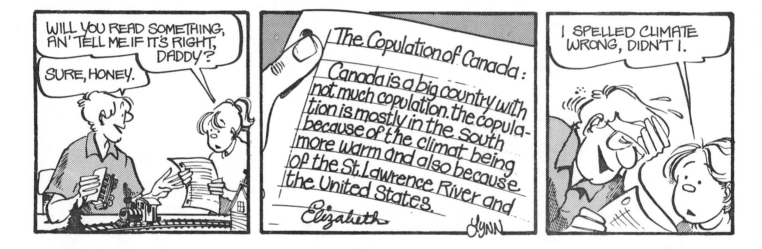

16

18

21

RUNNING A HOT-DOG STAND IS AN INTERESTING BUSINESS....

YOU STAND ON THE CORNER, WATCHING LIFE PASS BY LIKE AN ENDLESS PARADE.

AND YOU WONDER TO YOURSELF: "WHAT'S IT ALL ABOUT?"

PATTERSON!! LOOK BUSY!

WE'RE HERE TO MAKE A FEW BUCKS, REMEMBER?

UH, DAVE—YOU NEVER PAID ME FOR THE FOOTLONG!

SO. PUT IT ON MY TAB.

I CAN'T DO THAT, MAN—YOU OWE ME THREE BUCKS.

WELL, I'M KINDA LOW ON CASH.

DAVE, IF YOU DON'T PAY UP, I CAN CHARGE YOU WITH THEFT!

THEFT? FOR A LOUSY HOT DOG? GET REAL!

YOU GOT SOMETHING WITHOUT PAYING FOR IT. WHAT DO YOU CALL THAT?

HOW 'BOUT "A GIFT FOR A FRIEND"?

LISTEN, MIKE. WHO'S GONNA CARE IF YOU GIVE AWAY SOME OF THIS STUFF. THE GUY WHO OWNS THIS STAND WILL NEVER KNOW THE DIFFERENCE.

I'M YOUR FRIEND, RIGHT? WHAT'S WRONG WITH GIVING SOMETHING TO A FRIEND?

NOTHING—WHEN IT'S SOMETHING THAT BELONGS TO ME.

GET REAL. YOU GOT A LOTTA STUFF HERE. IF YOU DON'T SELL IT, YOU HAFTA CHUCK IT OUT. WHAT'S THE POINT IN TRASHING GOOD FOOD?

I DON'T KNOW.

BUT IT'S BETTER THAN TRASHING MY REPUTATION. —PAY UP!

27

38

41

48

Panel 1:
WE'RE SITTING HERE, TALKING ABOUT MIDDLE AGE, CAROL—AND LOOK AT ME!

IT'S WONDERFUL, EL. IT REALLY IS.

Panel 2:
EVERYONE I KNOW IS TALKING ABOUT CAREERS AND TRAVEL—AND I'M BACK TO DAY CARE AND DIAPER RASH!

ISN'T IT EXCITING?!!

Panel 3:
WHY IS IT THAT EVERY TIME I COMPLAIN ABOUT THIS PREGNANCY, MY FRIENDS TELL ME HOW LUCKY I AM!

WE'RE ALL SO HAPPY ABOUT IT. THAT'S ALL!

Panel 4:
REALLY?

SURE!

Panel 5:
IF IT HAD TO HAPPEN TO ONE OF US....WE'RE HAPPY IT'S YOU!!

Lynn

Panel 1:
AMAZING, ISN'T IT.—A FEW WEEKS AGO, THIS WAS JUST A TINY SEED—AND **NOW** LOOK AT HER!

Panel 2:
ALL I'VE DONE IS TAKE CARE OF HER, SEE THAT SHE'S WATERED REGULARLY, AND SHE JUST GROWS AND GROWS!

Panel 3:
EVERY DAY, SHE GETS A LITTLE BIGGER, A LITTLE ROUNDER, A LITTLE HEAVIER...

Panel 4:
...CAN WE TALK?

Lynn

Panel 1:
SPEAKING OF KIDS, THERE'S SOMETHING I WANT TO DISCUSS, ELLY...IT'S ABOUT BRIAN.

Panel 2:
HE'S NOT INTERESTED IN GIRLS. HE LIKES SPORTS AND SCHOOL, HE HAS LOTS OF FRIENDS—BUT HE HAS NO INTEREST IN GIRLS AT ALL! I'M SORT OF WORRIED.

Panel 3:
I KNOW HOW YOU FEEL, CAROL. I'M WORRIED ABOUT MICHAEL, TOO.

BECAUSE HE'S NOT INTERESTED IN GIRLS?

Panel 4:
NO....BECAUSE HE **IS**!!

Lynn

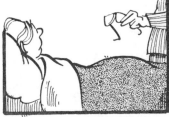

51

57

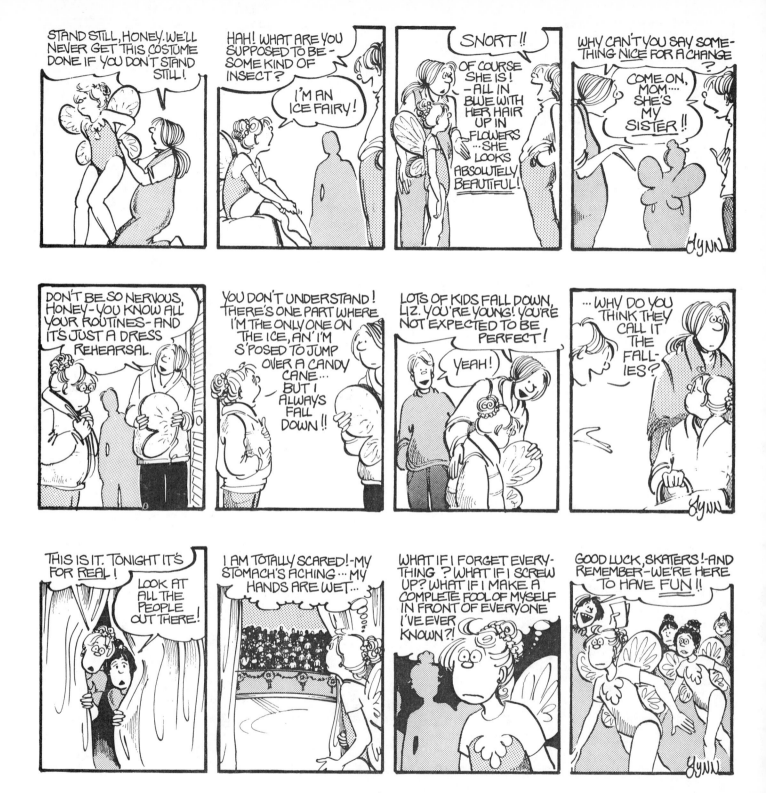

72

AND, HERE, SKATING TO THE THEME FROM "THE NUTCRACKER" ARE OUR OWN SUGARPLUM FAIRIES!

¿SNIFF¿ THEY ARE SO BEAUTIFUL! - ALL THOSE CHILDREN, MOVING TOGETHER ... PRACTICED, PRECISE ... LOOK AT THEIR FACES, SO FULL OF LIFE AND PROMISE.

- IT'S ONLY AN ICE SHOW, FOR HEAVEN'S SAKE! WHAT'S THE MATTER WITH ME? NOBODY ELSE IS FALLING APART OVER THIS!!

WHONK!!

CLAP CLAP CLAP CLAP CLAP CLAP CLAP!! CLAP

DID YOU LIKE IT? WAS IT OK? MAN, MY FEET ARE SWEATIN' - YOU WOULDN'T BELIEVE WHAT KAREN DID TO BRETT BEFORE HE WENT ON! SHE DUMPED A BOX OF NERDS DOWN HIS TIGHTS! CAN I HAVE SOME MONEY? - I'M STARVED! -

BOY, AM I EVER GLAD THAT'S OVER! I WAS SO SCARED, I THOUGHT I WAS GONNA BARF! - BUT I NEVER FELL ONCE! DIDJA CHECK OUT BRENNA? SHE STUFFED HER FRONT WITH KLEENEX -

WHY IS DAD STILL SITTING IN THE BLEACHERS?

.... HE DOESN'T WANT THE MAGIC TO END.

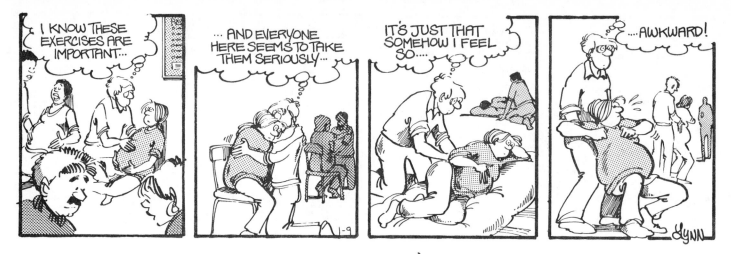

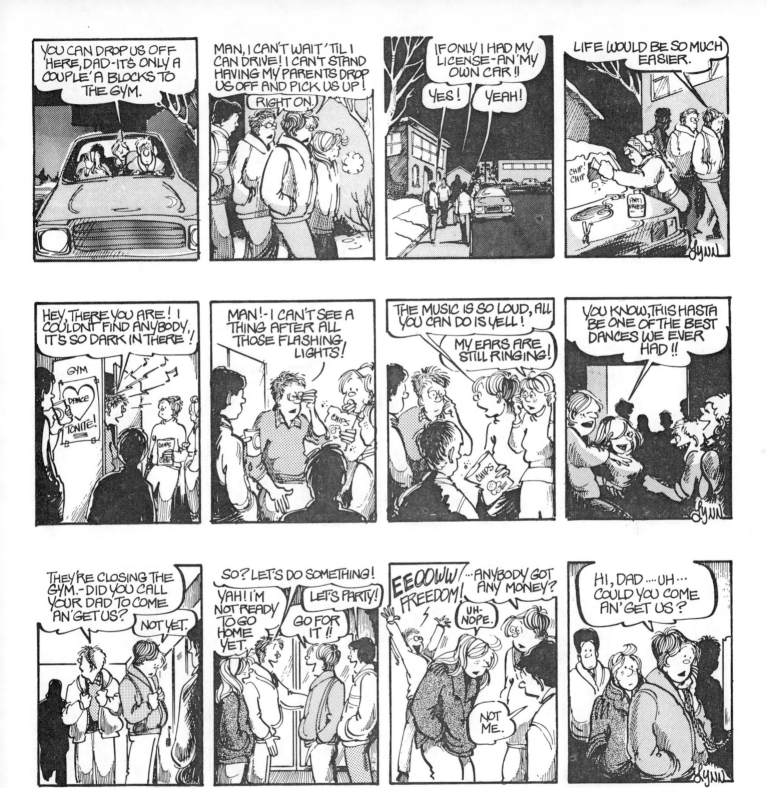

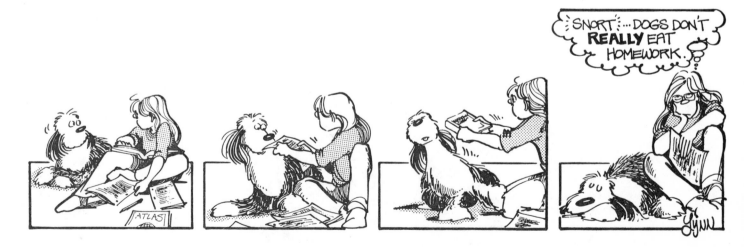

123

124

"How Beautiful You Are"
by Lynn Johnston

"How Beautiful You Are"

Lynn Johnston & Stabur Graphics are proud to offer a limited edition print of one of the more popular "For Better or For Worse" Sunday comic strips. Typical of all Lynn Johnston's work, this print captures one of the true episodes of life. Sure to touch a family-experienced heart! Each print is a six color, fine art reproduction printed on 100% acid-free, Saxony fine art paper, signed and numbered by Lynn Johnston! Hurry and order yours now due to limited print size of only 395. They are sure to sell out soon!

● Print Size: 14 1/2" x 17 1/2" ● Image Size: 9" x 13" ● Limited to 395
● Six Color ● Signed & Numbered ● Provided with Certificate of Authenticity
● Printed on 100% acid-free, Saxony Fine Art Paper

To order use the coupon provided below or for fastest service use your Visa, MasterCard, American Express, Discover or Diner's Club credit card and call our toll-free number!

Each lithograph only $59.95! (Plus $8.00 shipping and handling charge) 1-800-346-8940